Advance praise for *I Feel Insufferior:*

I Feel I   tive
about li: ach
chapter   **Date Due**   iese
feelings   en-
cy. If yo   JUL 1 0 2016   rist
instead   JUL 3 1 2016   ig a
defeated
            JUL 0 9 2017

                                                                 ı.D.
                                                                 sor
         P: OH
                                                                 ˈlor

I Feel *Insufferior*

New Hope for Real Change

May God abundantly bless you,

Melody Metzger

Melody Metzger, MC, MTC

I FEEL INSUFFERIOR
Copyright © 2015 by Melody Metzger

ISBN: 978-1-4866-1093-8   Printed in Canada

Word Alive Press
131 Cordite Road, Winnipeg, MB R3W 1S1
www.wordalivepress.ca

Library and Archives Canada Cataloguing in Publication

Metzger, Melody, author
    I feel insufferior : new hope for real change / Melody Metzger, MC, MTC.

Issued in print and electronic formats.
ISBN 978-1-4866-1093-8 (paperback).--ISBN 978-1-4866-1094-5 (pdf).--
ISBN 978-1-4866-1095-2 (html).--ISBN 978-1-4866-1096-9 (epub)

    1. Self-actualization (Psychology)--Religious aspects--Christianity.
I. Title.

BV4598.2.M48 2015   248.4   C2015-906854-1
                                           C2015-906855-X

Dedicated to my firstborn, Brianna

and God, for the inspiration.

Contents

1.

I Feel Insufferior!

WHEN MY DAUGHTER UTTERED THESE WORDS TO ME, MY FIRST thought was to correct her vocabulary. "Oh, you mean inferior, or insufficient, or inadequate, or insecure." Of course, I did empathize with and comfort her, though. I told her the truth of who she is. I told her how I see her. I told her how God sees her.

However, as I pondered the word she had used—insufferior—I immediately realized that I knew exactly how she felt. That word said so much and expressed what has become epidemic in today's society. It is a combination of all these fears—inferiority, insecurity, inadequacy, and insufficiency—adding up to low self-esteem. This was my child who is usually so bubbly, confident, outgoing, effervescent, and full of joy, but she was going through a rough time. Some people go through most of their lives with feelings of insecurity, inferiority, inadequacy, low self-esteem, and all the maladies that can accompany it. Others will only experience it temporarily.

Of course, I knew what she was feeling because I had spent most of my life fighting those very feelings. What she was experiencing had been modelled by me, as I had learned them from my mother, and so on and so on. The generational curses will continue as long as we allow them. Colossians 2:15 says, *"And having disarmed the powers and authorities, he made a public spectacle of them, triumphing over them by the cross"* (NIV). So why is it so hard to overcome? Why does it feel like such a daily struggle? Why do I recognize these traits in so many people, not only myself?

I hold a Masters in Therapeutic Counselling, and this is the underlying problem in most people who come to me for counsel. As I work with them and they start to get better, I often feel like a fraud, because I'm still struggling with these issues on a regular basis myself. Then I question whether they're really healed. Is it just temporary? Of course, I recognize that these thoughts come on my low days. In other words, on the days when I haven't taken authority over the lies. On the days when I feel weak. So why, with all my knowledge and training, and with the ability to help others, do I still have to fight this battle?

I have pondered and worked at these very questions for my whole career—for most of my life, in fact. Now I have taken steps to overcome them, and I'll share how with you in this book.

It is my calling to help people on the road to recovery. Emotional health belongs to all of us, but few of us actually live there. Yes, many appear confident and self-assured, but often those who exude the most confidence struggle inwardly to believe it. Most of us walk around with covers, a façade of well-being, cheerfulness, and confidence. Inside, we ask ourselves, "Did that sound stupid? Do I look like an idiot? Why can't I be like other people?"

Does this sound like you?

First, we need to understand what insecurity, inferiority, inadequacy, insufficiency, and low self-esteem are. From this point on, I will refer to all of these afflictions as "insufferiority." I fully believe we cannot overcome issues if we don't really understand what they are and where they come from.

I believe in delving into the roots of problems. Just like weeds, if we don't deal with the roots, they will only come back—usually multiplied. Dealing with surface issues, like the dandelion head, is like putting a bandage over an infected cut; it will only grow, spread, and worsen. It's usually painful to clean out that wound and kill the infection. It is the same with our emotions.

It's much easier to understand our emotional issues by comparing them to physical ones. The society we live in accepts physical illness and issues as things we can't help, and it's understood that we sometimes need help from others, such as medical professionals. Unfortunately, mental illness and emotional issues tend to be viewed as weaknesses, and sometimes people are shunned because of them. Many are afraid to reach out for help or seek counselling because there's still a lot of stigma attached. It's definitely better than it used to be, but I still have clients who are embarrassed. Most insurance companies cover counselling in employee benefit packages, but many people never claim them because they don't want others to know that they needed help. How sad.

Truly, this is insufferiority, a fear of man and what other people will think.

Understanding Insecurity, Inferiority, Insufficiency, Inadequacy, and Low Self-Esteem

What Is Insecurity?

SO LET'S GET TO THE ROOT OF THIS EPIDEMIC. WHAT IS insecurity? I could give you dictionary definitions, but if you're reading this book, chances are you are only too aware of the definitions. You perhaps believe that you're less than other people in some or all ways. You have a basic lack of confidence in yourself and your abilities. You don't feel secure or safe maybe. You are uncertain about your future, even for the day.

When I'm in big groups of people, I tend to feel more insecure. Why would this be? I'm definitely introverted, so this might contribute, but being introverted doesn't make me less than others or less capable. I do feel more comfortable in a one-on-one situation, and this is common with introverts. However, if I'm honest with myself, perhaps part of it is that there are fewer people to dispute what I'm saying or challenge me. So I must be insecure in what I'm saying. But really, I'm not. I fully believe what I profess. The underlying issue is still insecurity. Not that I believe it less, but that someone else might not believe me.

So what? Why should that matter? Nobody's going to believe everything another person says. We're all different, unique individuals with differing opinions, values, and views. That's what makes this world so wonderful and relationships so valuable. We do challenge each other, and this helps us to come to our own unique understandings and beliefs. I can counsel myself through problems, but why is my natural response still fear?

Do you relate? Well, the truth is that it's becoming less and less so for me, because I've worked through the insufferiority so much. I will teach you how to overcome as well.

Of course, I struggle sometimes. I'm human. I have also learned that I don't need to subject myself to certain situations. In fact, it's my insecurity that allows me to put myself in these situations. I'm often afraid to say no, and I believed that I *have* to go. Why? Because of my fear of what others may think or say.

Ugh, back to insecurity. It really is a vicious cycle.

I want to help you break that cycle and start living in freedom. Anxiety often leads to depression, and anxiety and depression cause many physical health problems. Ulcers, heart problems, hemorrhoids, digestive issues, headaches, and other conditions have been linked to stress. Anxiety and depression cause stress. Insecurity causes stress, anxiety, and depression. Do you want off this rollercoaster?

You can be free.

What Is Inferiority?

Do you believe that you're less important than other people? Perhaps you don't actually believe that when you challenge yourself, but perhaps you live as if you are less important. Do you see yourself as lower in rank than others?

Our society has a tendency to rank people, and we're supposed to respect those who are in authority over us. However, this isn't really the same thing as actually being inferior. Pastors, governments, and law enforcement officers are all above me in rank, but they're not more valuable than I am. This is hard for many of us to grasp.

The Bible tells us that we are all created equal.

> *There is neither Jew nor Gentile, neither slave nor free, nor is there male and female, for you are all one in Christ Jesus.*
> —Galatians 3:28, NIV

> *For there is no difference between Jew and Gentile—the same Lord is Lord of all and richly blesses all who call on him...*
> —Romans 10:12, NIV

As Christians, we are taught that we must be humble. *"God opposes the proud but gives grace to the humble"* (James 4:6, NLT). One of my favourite quotes is by C.S. Lewis, who said, "True humility is not thinking less of yourself; it is thinking of yourself less."[1] Wow, that makes such a difference.

Many Christians actually promote inferiority through a misunderstanding of what Christ taught us. Did Jesus think less of Himself than others? It might appear so, since He was willing to die for us, but in fact He was able to die for us because He was better than all of us. He was perfect. Jesus modelled self-confidence. He was assertive but kind, loving, and encouraging—and He always thought of Himself less than He did of others. He didn't think less of Himself, though.

Do you see the difference? Learning to be assertive is not in opposition to being humble. In fact, it is false humility to put yourself down or think less of yourself. Assertiveness is learning how to consider all people as equal. I'm truly assertive when I can put forth my point of view or desires while still considering and valuing other people's points of view and desires.

This is not the same as agreeing with everything someone else might say. I can disagree without disrespecting

---

1 C.S. Lewis, "Quotable Quote," *Goodreads*. Date of access: August 23, 2015 (http://www.goodreads.com/quotes/201236-true-humility-is-not-thinking-less-of-yourself-it-is).

them, which values their rights to have a differing opinion. An inferiority complex would cause me to believe that my opinion or desire is less important. Of course, there are times when I might choose to put someone else's desires in front of my own. This is humility, but I don't tell myself that it's because I'm less important. I am not inferior.

There are many people who are smarter, more talented, and have much more experience than I do in many capacities. This doesn't make them more important than I am, though. The Bible tells me that I am God's child (John 1:12), that I have been bought with a price (1 Corinthians 6:20), and that I am chosen (1 Peter 2:9). This is who you are, too. You're not inferior; you are a chosen, valuable, priceless treasure. I want to help you believe this and live it.

What Is Inadequacy and Insufficiency?

A common statement I hear from my clients is "I am inadequate." Where does this come from? Why do people think they're not good enough? The Bible tells me that I'm a branch of the true vine (John 15:5). John 15:7 says, *"But if you remain in me and my words remain in you, you may ask for anything you want, and it will be granted!"* (NLT) So all I have to do is remain in Him.

I do. I'm a practicing Christian, but sometimes I feel like it isn't enough. The enemy loves to tell us that we're not enough, that we're not acceptable. Jesus says that we are enough because He is enough. He paid the price for my freedom. That freedom includes the right to live as an heir, as the princess He created me to be.

So why do I often feel like I'm not enough, like I'm incompetent, like I'm lacking something? Well, in those instances I *am* lacking something—confidence, and perhaps faith to believe and receive God's promises. Or perhaps it's because of guilt for my many transgressions. Do you struggle with guilt? Many Christians are fighting guilt when they're struggling with confidence. The enemy loves to keep us trapped in guilt. I'll discuss this issue more in-depth later.

Ephesians 2:19–22 tells us,

Consequently, you are no longer foreigners and strangers, but fellow citizens with God's people and also members of his household, built on the foundation of the apostles and prophets, with Christ Jesus himself as the chief cornerstone. In him the whole building is joined together and rises to become a holy temple in the Lord. And in him you too are being built together to become a dwelling in which God lives by his Spirit. (NIV)

Wow! This is my heritage and yours. Do I always live as though God lives in me? If I truly believe and receive this truth, I would never doubt or feel inadequate.

I believe that guilt often keeps us from walking victoriously. Christ has already overcome everything, which means I have, too. It's time for me to receive it and live free. He is sufficient, and therefore I am sufficient. So are you.

What Is Low Self-Esteem?

Do you have respect for yourself and your abilities? Are you confident and satisfied in yourself? If not, you may be struggling with low self-esteem. If you struggle with feelings of inferiority, insecurity, inadequacy, or insufficiency, you likely have low self-esteem.

A few months ago, I came across a workbook for building self-esteem. I purchased a few and thought I might use them for my clients to work through. I wasn't surprised to find that most of my clients did, in fact, struggle with this very issue. People come to counselling for many different reasons, yet no matter what they come for, self-esteem issues show up as root problems when we start to look into their concerns and reasons for seeking counselling. I have not yet had a client say, "No, I don't think this will help me." This tells me that most people appear to be aware of the low-esteem struggle.

However, people don't come to counselling only to work on their self-esteem. This suggests that one's low self-esteem exists underneath the problems they're seeking help for.

What if we worked on our self-esteem before it led to all the problems it can cause in our lives? It would be kind of like eating healthy and exercising so that we don't get high blood pressure, cholesterol issues, heart disease, or cancer. The fact is that even if we eat extremely healthy and exercise, we're not immune to disease. If we struggle with inferiority, insecurity, inadequacy, or insufficiency, we are likely to have problems with anxiety and depression. This allows stress to wreak havoc in our bodies. Stress, anxiety, and depression leads to high blood pressure, cholesterol issues, heart disease, and cancer. And then we're right back to the start of that vicious cycle of destruction.

I don't believe God wants us to live like this. I do, however, believe that I have a part in changing this cycle in my life. Yes, Jesus can and will heal me, but I need to make changes in my life so that the same issues don't keep happening.

When someone is diagnosed with cancer or heart disease, often you see them making huge changes in their lives. Suddenly they're desperate enough to change their eating and exercise habits. Sometimes it's too late, but sometimes it really helps. And what about their mental attitudes? It's a proven fact that people who are positive and believe they will get better do so at a much greater percentage than those who give up. If someone has weight-loss surgery, but continues to eat according to their old habits, they will soon have the same problem again. That's why I feel confident some days and struggle other days. However, after learning how to change my behaviour, I have the tools to overcome. I can create new and healthier habits in my life.

I'll show you how to make these changes in your life, step by step. You do not have to feel insufferior!

Exercises

Be sure to fill out your answers fully and in detail. Use additional paper as required.

1.   In what ways do you feel insecure?

_____

_____

_____

_____

_____

2. Do you have an inferiority complex? How and when do you feel inferior to others?

_____

_____

_____

_____

_____

3 In what ways do you see yourself as inadequate?

_____

_____

_____

_____

_____

4. In what ways do you see yourself as insufficient?

_____

_____

_____

_____

_____

5. Is your self-esteem healthy, as God created you to be? What is your greatest struggle in the balance between self-confidence and humility?

_____

_____

_____

_____

_____

3.

Commitment and Basics

WHERE DO WE START IN ORDER TO CHANGE THIS CYCLE OF DEFEAT in our lives? Honestly, the answers are within each of us individually. We're all different, so our issues with insufferiority will be unique to us. That being said, some basic changes will make positive differences in all of our lives. The principles are the same, but we'll learn how to adapt them to our own personal strengths and weaknesses.

I encourage you to put your effort into each step, as it will prepare you for the one to follow. Do what will work for you the most in each step. Just make sure you do the work. Getting healthy does require work. Change doesn't happen on its own, so you will need to understand that if you want to make the changes I have discussed so far, it will require hard work and effort. Furthermore, it's important that you work on each step, even if the next one appears more applicable.

When I was younger, I really wanted to be able to dive, but I didn't think I would ever be able to. I'm not the most coordinated person and have never been good at sports. I never even learned how to swim. All of my friends could. Yes, I wanted to fit in, but I also loved the water. Once I was a teenager and working, I paid to put myself in swimming lessons. It was embarrassing to only be learning as a teenager, but I did it anyway because it was important to me.

While taking these lessons, I noticed that the pool management also offered an adult diving class. This was so enticing, but I didn't believe I would ever be able to make those beautiful dives I watched others perform. Somehow I overcame my fear and enrolled in the class. I prepared myself to be embarrassed, since everyone else would probably be better than me.

It was ten lessons. On the first day, the instructor started with the absolute basics. We learned how to walk on the diving board and where to place our feet. Well, I may be somewhat uncoordinated, but I can walk. I thought it a bit ridiculous to waste a whole lesson on this when I wanted to be able to gracefully float through the air and glide gently into the water without a splash. I did what the instructor said, though, and followed every direction. I soon realized that it did make a difference where I started, and with which foot. Of course, I had jumped in the water from a diving board before, but being able to go headfirst was the challenge, especially for it to look good and not hurt. Now I had to change the way I even jumped in the water.

This is what you'll be doing in your emotional life, too. We all develop habits, things we do without even thinking. Some of the habits you have developed are contributing to your insufferiority. You'll need to start with the basics in order to change your thinking about yourself and overcome your insufferiority.

Anyway, to continue my story, I did learn how to dive. In just a few lessons, I was doing swan dives and pikes, and it felt amazing. No, I didn't compete in the Olympics, but that wasn't my goal. I was so thrilled and amazed that I was able to perform these dives, and better than several others in my class.

That was when I learned the importance of starting with the basics, the importance of unlearning the bad habits I had already formed. In ten easy lessons, I learned how to dive. That was quite a feat for me. It was even more important, though, to learn to start with the basics. I don't dive much now, but I use this life lesson on a daily basis.

I encourage you to start by making a commitment to yourself to really work through this. You're worth it and your life will change in magnificent ways. Half the battle of doing anything is believing that you can really do it.

Do you have hopes, dreams, and goals? Does it sometimes feel like you will never achieve them? I can relate. I felt called to be a counsellor from the time I was a teenager, but I went to Bible College first to get a good grounding in the Word. I use this education every day, but after graduating I couldn't afford to continue with counsellor training. I thought I would work for a while and still go. But life happened. I got married and started a family, and there was no way for me to go back to school. I all but gave up on my dream. I would cry out to God and then let it go. I consoled myself, saying that perhaps God only ever wanted me to be there for my friends and family. I tried to let that be enough.

Then an amazing thing happened. God came through when I had completely given up—rather, when I finally laid myself down. This was truly a "let go and let God" situation. He provided the way, and I achieved my dreams and goals. However, I never gave up on believing in myself. I knew I would be able to counsel if I managed to find a way to get the training. Start to believe that you can accomplish your God-given goals!

Do you believe you can overcome your insecurity? Your inferiority complex? Your fear of man? Yes, I believe that much of our insufferiority comes back to a fear of man. If we weren't so concerned about what others think, we wouldn't have a reason to feel insecure or inadequate. This is very close to having a fear of judgment, because most of us plagued in this area are afraid of being judged by others. Is this true for you? Do you compare yourself to others all the time and think you are less able, capable, talented, smart, good-looking, etc.? This is low self-esteem, but would it be a problem if you had no one else to compare yourself to? Then there would be no one else to judge you. Only you can look at your life and decide the root causes of your problems.

For many, the problems stem from childhood, during which they didn't receive the affirmations they needed and deserved. Many parents get caught up in correcting their children and forget to tell them about everything they're doing right. I certainly failed in this area, and I've worked hard to change it now. My own parents were more critical than praising, as were their parents. I like to believe that it's getting better with each generation. My mother certainly did much better than her parents, from the stories I've heard.

The biggest changes started to happen for me when I realized, as an adult, that it was up to me. Blaming my parents might give me an excuse, but it didn't change anything. I realized that I didn't want to be that kind of parent. As a child, it was easy to say, "I will never treat my kids like that." However, once I was a parent, I had to acknowledge how often I was doing exactly the things that had been modelled to me. It isn't natural to do what we haven't learned. So I had to purposefully set about making the changes I wanted to see in my life and in my parenting. This is hard work, but my children were worth it to me.

Am I worthy of change? Are you? Some people actually answer this question negatively because their self-esteem is so low. When I felt that low, I thought about my children. I knew that they deserved better. I hope and pray that if you are that low, you have someone in your life for whom it is worth changing yourself. One of the hardest things for me was seeing my children struggle with low self-esteem and fear of man, because I knew this is what they had seen modelled by me. This gave me the courage and motivation to seek change in my life.

If you are reading this book, a part of you wants change. You want to get better, and you hope this can help you. Make a commitment to yourself right now to follow the steps and believe in yourself. You can change. God can change you, and He has led you to this book. This is part of your healing process.

It is important to note here that as you analyze yourself and look for the root causes of your issues, you might realize that some of these roots are the result of previous trauma or abuse. If this is the case, you may need professional counselling before you can proceed with overcoming your insufferiority.

Exercises

1. What are the root causes of your insufferiority?

_____

_____

_____

_____

2. Write out your commitment to yourself to overcome insufferiority and start living as God intended. (It is very important to make this commitment. You will need to remind yourself of your commitment when you hit tough times while working through this.)

_____

_____

_____

_____

3. As further reinforcement, write out all the negative ways in which insufferiority has affected your life. For example, what sort of things have you been too afraid to do?

_____

_____

_____

_____

_____

4. Lastly, how will your life be better after you have followed these steps and overcome your insufferiority?

_____

_____

_____

_____

_____

4.

Negative Thinking

WOULD YOU CALL YOURSELF AN OPTIMIST OR A PESSIMIST? I USED to be a confirmed pessimist. I truly believed that if I expected something to be good, I would always be disappointed, but if I didn't expect as much, I might be pleasantly surprised. I lived my life by this motto—and well, I got by.

This is an example of negatively controlled thinking. God doesn't want us to just get by. He wants us to live victoriously. We have been saved by grace. We have been bought with the highest price. We are king's children, heirs to the throne of God. We should be walking around with our heads held high, exuding the love of God, not hiding in defeat and shame and putting ourselves down.

After years of living by this motto, I heard a sermon on self-fulfilling prophecies. You know how you can hear the same message over and over and it makes sense but doesn't really sink in? But then, one day, God makes it real in your heart. It's like a light bulb goes on and the message becomes alive in your spirit. This is the rhema Word from God. He helped me see the truth in my negative outlook one day and I became an optimist. This was one of those immediate and drastic changes. Most are not so easy and fast, which is why I will guide you through the steps for change in the following chapters.

The words that we speak have power. I never before realized how much power there was in words. Every time I said something negative, I was actually pronouncing it to be so. This is a self-fulfilling prophecy, except it's a negative prophecy. How many times did I predict a negative outcome and actually accept it? Do you do this?

The enemy cannot hear our thoughts. He plants thoughts in our mind, but we have a choice of whether to receive them. However, he hears what we speak aloud and works to use it negatively in our lives. Matthew 18:18 states, *"Truly I tell you, whatever you bind on earth will be bound in heaven, and whatever you loose on earth will be loosed in heaven"* (NIV). We understand that this works for good things, but the enemy also uses it for the negative things we say. The laws and principles God has created are valid whether we believe them or not. Just like the law of gravity.

Did you know that when you say negative things about yourself, you are actually giving the enemy permission to work negatively in your life? It's like making an agreement with the devil. He works hard to make the lies true and this, of course, convinces us that our negative statements are true, which only reinforces the lie. 1 Peter 5:8 teaches us, *"Be alert and of sober mind. Your enemy the devil prowls around like a roaring lion looking for someone to devour"* (NIV).

We have a very real enemy, and he never gives up. Just as God neither slumbers nor sleeps (Psalm 121:4), neither does our enemy. However, do not be fearful of the devil, for as we learn in 1 John 4:4, *"You, dear children, are from God and have overcome them, because the one who is in you is greater than the one who is in the world"* (NIV). We have been equipped with every spiritual blessing (Ephesians 1:3). We have been given spiritual armour to fight all the wiles of the devil:

> *A final word: Be strong in the Lord and in his mighty power. Put on all of God's armor so that you will be able to stand firm against all strategies of the devil. For we are not fighting against flesh-and-blood enemies, but against evil rulers and authorities of the unseen world, against mighty powers in this dark world, and against evil spirits in the heavenly places.*
>
> *Therefore, put on every piece of God's armor so you will be able to resist the enemy in the time of evil. Then after the battle you will still be standing firm. Stand your ground, putting on the belt of truth and the body armor of God's righteousness. For shoes, put on the*

> *peace that comes from the Good News so that you will be fully prepared. In addition to all of these, hold up the shield of faith to stop the fiery arrows of the devil. Put on salvation as your helmet, and take the sword of the Spirit, which is the word of God.*
>
> —Ephesians 6:10–17, NLT

We must put on this armour and use it to refute every lie the devil throws at us. And we must stop giving him power in our lives. Yes, by speaking negatively about ourselves, we give him power. The devil wants us to wallow in self-pity. He wants us to be insecure. He wants us to feel inadequate. He wants us to believe that we are insufficient.

The devil tells you that you are inferior. As long as we believe these lies, we are not fulfilling God's purpose in our lives. We won't be able to function properly if we're beating ourselves up. We literally feel crippled when we feel insecure. The enemy loves this. He knows that we won't turn away from God, so he says, "That's fine. I'll keep you in a low, depressed, and crippled state so you won't be able to do any good for the kingdom." Do you relate to this? Are you giving the enemy power in your life?

What kinds of lies do you tell yourself? Believing that you're inferior is a blatant lie. You are not inadequate or insufficient. God has given us all the power and tools we need to succeed in what He has called us to do. We are all created uniquely and perfectly by the Father.

The problem is that some people have professed the lies so much that they actually believe them. The more they believe the lies, the more they live their lives as such.

Sadly, what we believe and profess about ourselves is also what we show to the rest of the world. We actually convince others that these lies are true, and they start to treat us accordingly. This only reinforces the lies in our own minds. Do you see how the enemy plants lies in our minds and sets about making them true?

I know people who repeatedly put themselves down. Do you? I certainly used to put myself down. If someone gave me a compliment, I would minimize or refute it. For example, when someone said that my top was nice, I would immediately say that it was old. Or I would tell them that I'd gotten it on sale, like I had to justify even having it. Why would I do that? Truly it comes from insecurity or inferiority, like I didn't think I was worthy of having a nice top. How sad is that? I wasn't even aware of this habit. It had become an automatic response.

Do you say things like that? I encourage you to become aware of your own self-talk. You can't stop the insufferiority until you're aware of how you perpetuate it. Yes, I'm going to be tough on you in order for you to truly break the cycle. It does start with you. If people treat you as less, it's because you believe you are less. I am going to help you to effect a change.

Our responses are so automatic that we have to work to recognize them. Do you remember my story in the last chapter about taking the diving class? Did you notice my automatic negative thinking? I had prepared myself to be embarrassed, because I thought everyone else would be better than me. Did you recognize that as a negative statement when you read it? I actually left it in there to see if you would. Why would I just assume and expect to be embarrassed? Why would I expect that everyone else would be better than me? What a defeating thought. That was how I was living my life then.

Do you say or think things like this? Are you aware of it? I challenge you to carry a notebook and write down each negative statement you make or think about yourself. It's one of the questions at the end of this chapter. If you truly want to overcome your insufferiority, do the exercises. Change will come, but it is hard work. You have lived your life thus far with this malady, and it will require effort to change.

Another lie is the fear of judgment, which can be so powerful that it causes us to miss out on many things we want to do. Have you ever declined an invitation because of a fear of judgment? Or have you missed appointments or meetings you really needed to be at?

One of my clients—let's call him Jeff—told me that he wasn't able to go up an escalator one day because there were people sitting on a bench at the top, and they were staring at him. Jeff said they were looking at him and judging him.

"Why do you think they were staring at you?" I asked.

"I didn't know. Maybe it was the way I was dressed."

He had been dressed completely fine. In fact, he had taken extra care that day because he was going out with friends later.

I'm familiar with the place he was talking about, having been there before. At the top of the escalator is an open hallway, and there are some public benches opposite the escalator. People can sit there while waiting for their appointments, or perhaps just to rest. I explained that sometimes when I'm deep in thought, my eyes are open, but I'm not seeing anything in particular. I'm caught up in my own thoughts. Sometimes my kids will ask, "Why are you staring at me like that? Why are you giving me that look?" When that happens, I'm completely unaware of where my gaze is focused. My look is probably relevant to my thought process, but it can be disconcerting for the object of my gaze. But it's not in the least judgmental. I wanted to give Jeff some perspective and alternate conclusions to draw.

When we're insecure, we tend to automatically make negative assumptions, and they're often wrong. If we dwell on them, we convince ourselves of things that aren't true. The more we do this, the more it becomes a habit. Some of us become quite paranoid!

Imagine that you're just sitting somewhere, like at a park, and everything is quiet and calm around you. Then a bird happens to fly in and dig for a worm. You automatically watch it, right? Your eyes are drawn to the different thing, whatever it may be. Are you judging the bird? No, there was simply a change in the environment surrounding you, and so that's what you look at.

The people at the top of the escalator didn't know Jeff and probably had no reason to judge him. Most likely, they were not judging him at all. They may not have even given him a second thought. Jeff's fear and insufferiority caused him to feel panic, and he allowed it to have a negative impact on him—an impact so great that he was unable to continue with his plans. The people whom Jeff had perceived as "staring" at him hadn't caused his problem; rather, it had been Jeff's own interpretation.

Do you see how we do actually have control over our own perceptions and reactions? I suggest that you challenge these kinds of automatic thoughts. I will teach you how to challenge them to the point where they're not the norm for you anymore. We will change the habit. Yes, it is in fact a habit, and it is changeable. You can overcome and live free of this fear.

Exercises

1. What lies do you tell yourself? Give this some serious thought and be honest with yourself. Write them down and we will work on them later.

_____

_____

_____

_____

_____

2. Do you have repetitive negative thoughts? What are they?

_____

_____

_____

_____

_____

3. Can you think of a self-fulfilling prophecy you have professed over yourself?

_____

_____

_____

_____

_____

4. Do you struggle with fear of judgment or fear of man? In what ways? What is the most crippling fear for you?

_____

_____

_____

_____

_____

5.

Psychological Sabotage

I TALKED ABOUT RANK AND HUMILITY IN CHAPTER TWO. NOW I want to talk to you about how we rank ourselves. I believe that we "slot" ourselves psychologically without even being aware of it. We automatically assess our opponents, or the people we're around or who we're going to be up against, in our day-to-day lives. Just as an athlete assesses their opponents for strength and size we do so mentally and emotionally, based on our strengths and weaknesses. We size up the people in our lives to decide whether we're emotionally or mentally stronger than them or better able to overtake them.

Social anxiety is probably among the biggest fears we struggle with, whether we acknowledge it or not. For most of us, this happens subconsciously; we're not even aware of it. Becoming more aware of ourselves and the people around us is the first step towards overcoming the ways in which we limit ourselves. I think we "slot" ourselves against each other.

Here's a good example of this. I once played a word game with someone. I'll call her Jane for the purposes of anonymity. Psychologically, I see myself as a little bit stronger than Jane. In this particular word game, I had been beating everyone and was feeling pretty cocky about it. My husband had played against several others, too, and had commented that Jane was very good. He had suggested that she would be my match and was excited to watch us play against each other.

I was actually a little bit afraid, because I really liked being the champion. Duh, who doesn't? However, we finally did play against each other—and she was beating me. I realized that perhaps I really had met my match in this game.

However, I still saw myself as psychologically stronger than Jane. This means that I knew she struggled with insufferiority a little more than I did. So when we had a conversation about our game, I told her that I hadn't played very well. I hadn't played my best. I further added that she probably needed the win more than I did. Yes, as you can see, I became really mean. I psychologically sabotaged her. Jane, being weaker psychologically and looking up to me, agreed with that assessment and allowed it to affect her. After that, and for the remainder of the game, she was unable to play as well. I did eventually win that game, even though she had been more than a hundred points ahead of me at one point and had every opportunity to beat me.

It was a hollow victory, though. I had taken advantage of her weakness. While this had probably happened subconsciously at first, a part of me had known that what I was doing was wrong, and I had to repent of it. Furthermore, I had to apologize to her. I probably damaged her through my own selfish ambition. I had to be accountable for this. So I did repent before God, and I apologized to her. This was psychological slotting. No, I'm not proud of this at all.

The truth is that I often psychologically slot myself lower than my counterparts. Since I set myself lower in my own mind, I don't achieve many of the things I want to, simply by my own self-imposed limitations. Have you ever done that? The key is to recognize this and learn why we do it. We can accept our limitations and then learn to overcome them.

We need to recognize that we are all equal on this earth. We need to find out what God wants for us, and sometimes it's not about who's physically, mentally, spiritually, or emotionally stronger. It's about what God wants to achieve. It's His goals that matter, not our own personal gain. He has chosen the weaker, the lesser, and the poor to be used in His service.

1 Corinthians 1:27 says, *"But God chose the foolish things of the world to shame the wise; God chose the weak things of the world to shame the strong"* (NIV). Why is that? Don't you think it's because the weaker people are more humble? Also, they are perceived as least

likely to succeed. The next verse says, *"God chose things despised by the world, things counted as nothing at all, and used them to bring to nothing what the world considers important"* (NLT). Because of this, the lesser ones will depend on God, glorifying Him. *"For when I am weak, then I am strong"* (2 Corinthians 12:10, NIV).

I believe God has chosen to use me at times simply because I'm willing, because I'm available, not because I'm able. Most of the time when God does use me, it's when I am the most unprepared. Or at least when I *feel* the most unprepared. I then have to totally rely on His strength and wisdom. When I think I'm prepared and ready for something, it often falls apart, and that's because I was trying to do it in my own strength. I cannot do it in my own strength. I can only do it in His strength. *"'Not by might nor by power, but by my Spirit,' says the Lord Almighty"* (Zechariah 4:6, NIV). So when we see ourselves as less than an opponent, whether it's another person or an idea, we psychologically sabotage ourselves. Or sometimes we psychologically sabotage other people, as I did in the incident with Jane.

Don't you think God would have us view each other as equals, as He created us? I know for certain that He didn't guide my behaviour toward Jane. Of course, He's always with me and willing to guide me, but I do have free will, and I exercised it for wrong in that instance. Luckily for me, Jesus paid the price and I was forgiven when I repented. I'm sure God used this as a lesson to teach me to do better going forward. I pray that He somehow uses it for good in Jane's life, too.

Mark 12:31 tells me, *"The second [commandment] is this: 'Love your neighbor as yourself.' There is no commandment greater..."* (NIV). Philippians 2:3 says, *"Do nothing out of selfish ambition or vain conceit. Rather, in humility value others above yourselves..."* (NIV). There's that word again—humility. So taking into consideration what we learned about humility—that it means thinking of ourselves less, not less of ourselves—wouldn't you agree that God desires that we be confident in ourselves, but not prideful, putting ourselves above others? There is a fine line, but I believe it is crucial to find the balance. It's crucial for our well-being and self-esteem, as well as for our spiritual welfare.

Of course, when we're in competition, it's healthy to size up our opponents and recognize our own abilities and limitations. God has gifted us each differently. He wants us to use the gifts He has given us to fulfill the purposes He created us for. If I decided to compete in the Olympics, it would be out of God's plan for my life, as He did not gift me in this area. I would soon feel defeated, as I'm not able to perform well enough athletically. The experience might cause me to see myself as inadequate, inferior, or insufficient. I would be trying to live outside of God's will for my life. Again, lucky for me, I have no desire to compete athletically in anything.

I think God gives us desires for the areas He has gifted us in. I receive the most unbelievable fulfillment when my clients overcome and find healing in counselling. It's the most amazing gift from God to witness these changes taking place in their lives. It's such an extreme privilege to work with His dear children. He is the healer, and the most important things I do toward counselling are make myself available and ask for His wisdom and guidance for each and every client. I know that my training and knowledge is part of it, but He provided the way for me to gain it.

God brings what I need to my remembrance and speaks through me to help the client. I know that God doesn't really need me; He could just as well use someone else or speak directly to each client. He chooses to bless me in this area as I'm obedient to fulfilling His purpose for my life. I am confident in my knowledge and abilities, but also mindful that it's only possible through His blessing. I view this as a healthy balance.

I would also like to comment here on worthiness. A common issue that comes up in counselling is the belief that we are unworthy to be used of God, be forgiven, or be blessed. Let me tell you something: we are all unworthy on our own, but that's why Jesus paid the ultimate price.

I started this chapter with a huge admission of wrongdoing. I then proceeded to give you an example of how God has used me in counselling, and how He has blessed me. Does that sound contradictory? I struggled with this for a long time, until I learned to forgive myself. This is very hard to do. It's one thing to apologize to someone else and ask forgiveness. It's another thing to ask God's forgiveness, because we sometimes struggle to receive it.

The question of forgiving ourselves comes up repeatedly. How could I just go forward after I'd done damage to Jane? I hate some of the things I've done in the past, and I'm sure you have situations you aren't proud of either. We all do. This is where guilt comes in, and it has the power to defeat us. God doesn't cause guilt; the enemy does. God convicts us through the Holy Spirit and moves us toward repentance. He always provides the way forward. Guilt leaves us crippled.

The greatest help to me in this area was the story of David. Wow, what a sinner he was! He committed adultery and murder, just to mention a couple. Yet God called David a man after his own heart.

> *But God removed Saul and replaced him with David, a man about whom God said, "I have found David son of Jesse, a man after my own heart. He will do everything I want him to do."*
> —Acts 13:22, NLT

There is no one else in the Bible whom God has said this of. I've pondered this much. David did do much good, too, and the lineage of Christ comes through David.

Why would God choose him? In my study of David, I have recognized that David had a repentant heart. In Psalm 51 (NLT), David repents for his actions:

Have mercy on me, O God,
because of your unfailing love.
Because of your great compassion,
blot out the stain of my sins.
Wash me clean from my guilt.
Purify me from my sin.
For I recognize my rebellion;
it haunts me day and night.
Against you, and you alone, have I sinned;
I have done what is evil in your sight.
You will be proved right in what you say,
and your judgment against me is just.
For I was born a sinner—
yes, from the moment my mother conceived me.
But you desire honesty from the womb,
teaching me wisdom even there.
Purify me from my sins, and I will be clean;
wash me, and I will be whiter than snow.
Oh, give me back my joy again;
you have broken me—
now let me rejoice.
Don't keep looking at my sins.
Remove the stain of my guilt.
Create in me a clean heart, O God.

Renew a loyal spirit within me.
Do not banish me from your presence,
and don't take your Holy Spirit from me.
Restore to me the joy of your salvation,
and make me willing to obey you.
Then I will teach your ways to rebels,
and they will return to you.
Forgive me for shedding blood, O God who
saves;
then I will joyfully sing of your forgiveness.
Unseal my lips, O Lord,
that my mouth may praise you.
You do not desire a sacrifice, or I would offer
one.
You do not want a burnt offering.
The sacrifice you desire is a broken spirit.
You will not reject a broken and repentant
heart, O God.
Look with favor on Zion and help her;
rebuild the walls of Jerusalem.
Then you will be pleased with sacrifices offered
in the right spirit—
with burnt offerings and whole burnt offerings.
Then bulls will again be sacrificed on your altar.

I love this prayer and pray it often when I feel convicted of something. I even used it to discipline my children, requiring them to learn it when they had done wrong. It's obvious that David is truly repentant and that it comes from his heart. This is what God wants from us.

From that time on Jesus began to preach, "Repent, for the kingdom of heaven has come near."

—Matthew 4:17, NIV

So watch yourselves. "If your brother or sister sins against you, rebuke them; and if they repent, forgive them.

—Luke 17:3, NIV

Produce fruit in keeping with repentance.
—Matthew 3:8, NIV

Repent, then, and turn to God, so that your sins may be wiped out, that times of refreshing may come from the Lord...

—Acts 3:19, NIV

God exalted him to his own right hand as Prince and Savior that he might bring Israel to repentance and forgive their sins.

—Acts 5:31, NIV

...yet now I am happy, not because you were made sorry, but because your sorrow led you to

repentance. For you became sorrowful as God
intended and so were not harmed in any way
by us.

—2 Corinthians 7:9, NIV

Did you see those words—"as God intended"? God desires us to repent so that He can forgive us. He does not see us as unworthy. He sees us through the veil of the cross. That means that He sees us as worthy, forgiven, and perfect, because He sees us after the sacrifice of Christ was applied. You are not unworthy. I am not unworthy. So if we are not unworthy, there's no reason to psychologically sabotage ourselves. We all have different strengths and weaknesses, but that doesn't make one better than the other. So why should we fear what others think of us?

I believe that David was so successful because he learned the art of forgiving himself and receiving God's forgiveness. He didn't allow his past sins to hinder him going forward. The enemy loves to keep us riddled with guilt so we cannot go forward and do what God is asking of us. Satan knows that I won't turn from God, so I think he says, "Fine, I'll just keep her busy at the cross and she won't do any good for the kingdom." I totally used to do this. I felt guilty (remember: guilt is not from God), so I continued to pray and repent over and over, as if my repeated bugging would make the difference.

I hate when my kids do this. When they continue to bug me for something, it never propels me to say yes, not after I've already said no. But you see, that's the difference: God hasn't said no, so why do we need to keep asking for something He's already given us? My kids never ask twice when I say yes. God said yes. He forgave us and provided a way for us to be free. We are free from sin and condemnation. *"Therefore, there is now no condemnation for those who are in Christ Jesus..."* (Romans 8:1, NIV).

There came a time when I repeatedly asked forgiveness for the same thing, and I heard God say to me, "Get up now and go do what I've asked." David was obedient to what God asked of him, and he was a man after God's own heart. David didn't allow his sin to hold him back, and therefore he accomplished much for the Kingdom. David didn't psychologically slot himself as lower than his adversaries. He didn't compare himself to others and allow it to affect him negatively. David probably wouldn't have overcome Goliath if he had started to doubt, saying, "But God, I am so small. You can use one of my brothers, or any of the other soldiers who are bigger and stronger than I am." No, David put his trust in God. David was obedient to the call of God on his life and didn't worry about the circumstances or his own limitations.

One more point: David didn't allow a fear of man to hold him back from doing what God had asked him to. He was jeered at and scoffed upon from both sides. Much of our own perceived mocking actually comes from our own minds. Sometimes it's real, too. David's was very real. He was scoffed at by Goliath, his enemy and adversary.

Goliath mocked him mercilessly. Goliath was trying to psychologically sabotage David. Furthermore, David was scoffed at by his brothers and fellow Israelites. These were the very people who should have supported and encouraged him, but they scoffed and jeered, too. In effect, they were prepared to lose David that day.

Would you allow one of your children to go up against such a giant? Would you be willing to sacrifice your child that way? I don't think I could. The Israelites were relying on man. They were looking for a man who could beat this giant. That's the problem; they were looking to man, not to God, to defeat their enemy. David was fully reliant upon God. He went forth in faith and trust, in spite of opposition from both sides, knowing very well that he couldn't do it in his own strength.

I have to add here that God *directed* David to do this. I'm not encouraging you to take on any giants unless you know God is directing you in your circumstance. Pray James 1:5 for wisdom in every situation.

Exercises

1. Have you ever psychologically sabotaged yourself? How?

_____

_____

_____

_____

_____

2. Have you ever psychologically sabotaged someone else? If so, how?

_____

_____

_____

_____

_____

3. Do you sometimes see yourself as unworthy? Take some time to ask God how He sees you. Write out His answer. (You will need more paper.)

_____

_____

_____

_____

_____

4. Do you have a repentant heart like David? Ask God if there are areas in your life that you have not repented of, and how to receive His forgiveness.

_____

_____

_____

_____

_____

5.   Do you struggle with forgiving yourself? What steps can you take to move forward in the giants God is asking you to slay, in His strength?

_____

_____

_____

_____

_____

6.

Encouragement and Affirmation

MY PASTOR OFTEN USES THE ANALOGY OF THE GROWTH OF flowers to describe our spiritual lives. He teaches that a seed must die before it can grow into a flower. The seed dies and lies dormant in the ground. It appears to be dead, but in fact this is how it reproduces. It can take years, but that seed grows a bit each season and then dies again in the winter months. However, it's not really dead. In the springtime, in the newness of life, it grows again and produces new seed. It eventually blossoms into fragrant beauty. Our spiritual lives are the same. We grow during our darkest times. This is when God does His deepest work in our hearts and lives, even though we don't see it, just like with the seed. We are strengthened, renewed, and then produce good fruit.

The Bible teaches us of the lilies of the field; they toil not, and neither do they spin (Matthew 6:28). This miraculous phenomenon just happens. Well, it doesn't just happen. God causes it to happen. He created life to continue this way. God waters the seed. He provides the sunlight. God encourages the seed to grow and produce life. A child who's often criticized does not prosper. However, one who feels loved, accepted, and encouraged feels confident, which empowers him to explore, create, learn, and try new things. The more he is willing and able to try without fear of failure, the more he will succeed.

How often have you been afraid to try things because of a fear of failure? Fear of man's judgment? Do you encourage others to go forth with their dreams and goals? What about yourself? I always thought that I did, but I've become more aware of how often I do not. Since I suffered from insufferiority, my negativity came across in my thoughts and speech without my being aware of it.

I've always thought that it's my job to correct my children. This is true, of course. The Bible teaches us to correct our children. Proverbs 22:6 says, *"Train up a child in the way he should go: and when he is old, he will not depart from it"* (KJV). Proverbs 13:24 says, *"Whoever spares the rod hates their children, but the one who loves their children is careful to discipline them"* (NIV). I mean, if I don't point out where they are erring, who will?

Recently, I have realized that sometimes when I'm quick to point out their faults, it's maybe more about my fear of what others will think of me, that I didn't do a good job. Ouch! That's a tough truth to face. Of course, it's in my children's best interests, too, but how many times do they just need my encouragement? My acceptance and love in spite of their mistakes?

Parenting is truly the hardest job on earth. God is the most amazing parent to me. He loves me and accepts me no matter how many times I fail. He knows that I'm well aware of my failings and mistakes. He knows that I need love and encouragement to pick myself back up and try again. And this, of course, is what my children need most from me.

One of the biggest struggles in my life is judgment. I often feel judged by others, and this cripples me. I have prayed for God to convict certain people of their judging nature. Seriously, I have. I often feel criticized, not encouraged. How do I rise above it and continue on in what God has called me to do? When sincerely seeking God on this matter, He reminded me of Matthew 7:1, which says, *"Do not judge, or you too will be judged"* (NIV). I had been using this verse to convict and point out the failure of others in this area. God, in His gentle love and kind conviction, said to me, "If you're feeling judged, perhaps you are being judgmental." Big ouch!

I realized that the first place in which I was guilty was judging others for being judgmental. God says in Matthew 7:5, *"You hypocrite, first take the plank out of your own eye, and then you will see clearly to remove the speck from your brother's eye"* (NIV). I realized that when I focus on removing my own plank, working on how not to judge others, I don't see the plank in my brother's eye so readily. In fact, I realize that God is their judge and will work on their faults. It's not even my place.

Furthermore, I know and fully believe that we can only work on one thing at a time. My family often wishes I were more this or that. I'm aware of other things I need to work on, but God is currently teaching me more of something else. By the same token, I can give more patience and understanding to the ones who offend me. God is working on something else in them and will eventually get to this other area that's bugging me so much. It's not my place to correct them. I further realized that my own insufferiority caused me to perceive negatively much of what others said. Often they weren't even judging me at all; it was only my tainted perception.

Of course, in the case of my children, I do have a responsibility to teach them better when they do things that are obviously wrong. However, I've learned to pick my battles, so to speak. God has taught me that it is okay to let some things go.

When I was a child, I remembered thinking that I was going to be in big trouble for the bad things I did. But sometimes my mom didn't get mad at me for it. Instead she showed compassion. Wow! Why do you think this is such a big memory to me? It didn't happen often and it was a special gem. I want my kids to have memories like this, of times when I showed grace instead of correction. That's what God does for me frequently.

What do you think would happen in our world if everyone encouraged instead of criticized? What if people only pointed out the good I do instead of how much I fail? What if I only pointed out the good in the people in my sphere of influence, instead of harbouring the hurt and pain they've caused me? Sometimes I hold grudges for how rude, insensitive, and bigoted other people are. In fact, when I focus on others' hypocrisy, I am the one being rude, insensitive, and bigoted. So again, this gives me more to work on and change in my own life.

Sometimes, it feels like I will never get there. And where is "there" anyway? Why do we have this constant goal to improve? Even this can be wrong motivation. Is it about perfection? How frustrating! Even when I'm trying to do better and improve myself, correcting my faults, I can be doing it for the wrong reasons. I don't want to be perfect, but I recognize that a perfectionist attitude creeps in sometimes. Will this ever end? What is God asking of me?

In the end, I believe it comes down to attitude and motivation. Perfection for the sake of being perfect is not perfect, because it arises from a wrong motive. Is my quest for perfection partly prompted by fear of what others will think of me? This takes me back to the judgment issue. So, judging others is wrong and will bring judgment upon me, but living in fear of others' judgment is also wrong. Sometimes it just seems like an endless circle. The more I try to do right, the more I fail. The apostle

Paul wrote it best in Romans 7:19: *"For I do not do the good I want to do, but the evil I do not want to do—this I keep on doing"* (NIV).

God has given me an understanding I can work with, one that I would like to share with you. God looks upon us in our finished state. He sees us as perfect, because we will be when He's finished working on us. That's why He can forgive my repeated failings in the same areas, and of course because of Calvary. He knows that while I keep repeating the same mistakes, as long as I repent and receive His forgiveness, He will continue to work on me to bring me toward perfection.

Philippians 1:6 says that *"He who began a good work in you will perfect it until the day of Christ Jesus"* (NASB). I have heard it said that once we are perfect, God takes us home to be with Him. I'm not sure this is biblical, but I can see the merit to it. I do, in fact, look toward receiving my heavenly inheritance and going home to be with Jesus, but I have so much to do here on earth first.

So why am I in such a rush to be perfect? This is another topic entirely. What I have learned is that only God perfects me, and He does it in His own perfect timing, methods, and order. When I'm striving, I usually don't succeed. I get so focused on what I don't want to do that I usually end up doing exactly that. Can you relate?

The enemy loves to beat me up and remind me of all my failings. God loves to remind me of all His successes. Yes, they are His successes. I usually pray for Him to help me and then set about trying to correct my problems myself. God must really chuckle when He watches my childlike attitude. I remember praying for God to help me overcome in some areas and then eventually giving up, thinking I couldn't do it. Later, God reminds me of this prayer and takes me back to where I was then.

As I honestly reflect, I can see that I have changed over time. The changes actually took place when I gave up and stopped trying to bring about the change myself. He worked the changes in me as I put my focus on Him. I didn't actually give up; I let go. You've probably heard the saying "let go and let God." There is great wisdom in this, as only God can bring about changes in my life. He's constantly working for good in me.

One of my favourite Bible verses is Psalm 46:10: *"Be still, and know that I am God."* Have you ever broken down the original Hebrew words of a verse to gain a better understanding of it? When you do so with this verse, it reads more like: "Let go, cease striving, be still, relax, and understand... know in your heart of hearts that only I am God, and only I can take care of this problem for you." Wow! That puts a whole new perspective on things for me.

I have a plaque in my office that someone gave me. It reads: "Good morning, this is God. I will be handling all of your problems today. I will not require your help." I love this plaque and find that it often gives me great comfort. However, sometimes I ponder if this is actually biblical. My dad always told me, "God helps those who help themselves." This is my husband's philosophy as well. So many of the sayings we're raised with and accept in society aren't actually what God would say.

So how do I bring it all into alignment? The simplest answer is to ask God. I fully believe that sometimes He would have me trust in Him and not try to work on things myself. At other times, I definitely do have a part. How do I know the difference? He is always available to answer my questions if I take the time to listen. Laziness and slothful behaviour is a sin, but not taking time to relax is sinful, too. He commanded me to rest and take care of my body so that I don't burn out. I have found that when I feel the most stressed and cannot handle everything that's on my plate, I'm likely trying to do things that God didn't ask me to do. Jesus was never rushed or stressed, yet He accomplished more than any man ever.

So, with all of this in consideration, how do I become more encouraging and less critical and judgmental of others? What do I do when I feel criticized and judged by others? How do I pick myself up and move forward when I feel crippled by a lack of support from those who are supposed to love me? How do I act perfectly in an imperfect world?

First of all, I've learned that I don't need to receive and accept another's judgment or criticism of me. I also don't have to rebuke them or point out how wrong they are. This accomplishes nothing, except perhaps to drive a gulf between me and my loved one. Not accepting and receiving this judgment simply means not acknowledging it to myself. I usually do check in with God and do some self-analysis to determine if there is some merit to the complaint. If there is, then of course I can try to rectify it. This will require me to seek God and ask His help in rectifying the change. If I've hurt someone, I need to repent and apologize appropriately. I'm not actually talking about these kinds of offenses. We all make mistakes and hurt people and need to make it right. I'm talking about the criticisms of our character from those well-meaning individuals who love to point out our weaknesses and flaws. You know, the comments that actually hinder us rather than move us forward.

When frustrated with my parenting, my children have at times made comments like "Some counsellor you are!" This is very hurtful to me, even though it's only said out of rebellion. The enemy loves to tell me it is true. Such statements will never help me to be a better counsellor, but they will cause me to second-guess myself. When I feel put down, I feel insecure. When I'm insecure, I'm less confident. When I'm less confident, I'm less likely to succeed. This isn't a good recipe for success before I go into a session with a client.

So how do I overcome this? First of all, I recognize that God is the true counsellor and that I am only the vessel He has chosen for this client. I am His tool, the mouth through which He might choose to speak—if I am willing and available. God has chosen to give me a blessing through each and every client He brings to me. I am trained and registered and have all the right tools as a counsellor. However, the more I learn, the less I feel equipped. There are so many therapeutic approaches, so how can I know which one is best in any given circumstance? I can't figure it out in my own human mind, but God can. He knows what each client needs and brings the right training to remembrance at the right time. So I pray for wisdom before each and every session. I pray according to James 1:5: *"If any of you lacks wisdom, you should ask God, who gives generously to all without finding fault, and it will be given you."* This gives me peace, which gives me confidence, which helps me feel successful. My confidence is in God, of course, not myself.

I have learned that God is my judge, not man. Therefore, I don't have to receive the criticism and judgment of man. Furthermore, I have learned to affirm myself. I don't have to give in to my insecurities. I overcome negative self-talk by telling myself truth. What is truth? Scripture is truth. *"Then you will know the truth, and the truth will set you free"* (John 8:32, NIV).

Who does Scripture say I am? God has given us a clear picture of who He created us to be, of how He sees us. If we listen to the enemy, he tells us that we aren't good enough, but God says that I am His child.

But as many as received him, to them gave he power to become the sons of God, even to them that believe on his name...
—John 1:12, KJV

God chose me and appointed me to bear fruit.

You did not choose Me but I chose you, and appointed you that you would go and bear fruit, and that your fruit would remain, so that whatever you ask of the Father in My name He may give to you.
—John 15:16, NASB

I have been forgiven and justified by Him. He gives me peace.

Therefore being justified by faith, we have peace with God through our Lord Jesus Christ...
—Romans 5:1, KJV

I am a new creation and minister of reconciliation.

Therefore if anyone is in Christ, he is a new creature; the old things passed away; behold, new things have come. Now all these things are from God, who reconciled us to Himself through Christ and gave us the ministry of reconciliation, namely, that God was in Christ reconciling the world to Himself, not counting their trespasses against them, and He has committed to us the word of reconciliation.

Therefore, we are ambassadors for Christ, as though God were making an appeal through us; we beg you on behalf of Christ, be reconciled to God.

—2 Corinthians 5:17–20, NASB

Jesus said that I am His friend.

No longer do I call you slaves, for the slave does not know what his master is doing; but I have called you friends, for all things that I have heard from My Father I have made known to you.

—John 15:15, NASB

He makes me complete.

...and in Him you have been made complete, and He is the head over all rule and authority.

—Colossians 2:10, NASB

Nothing and no one can separate me from God's love.

Who shall separate us from the love of Christ?
shall tribulation, or distress, or persecution, or
famine, or nakedness, or peril, or sword?
—Romans 8:35, KJV

I am free from condemnation.

Who then will condemn us? No one—for Christ
Jesus died for us and was raised to life for us,
and he is sitting in the place of honor at God's
right hand, pleading for us.
—Romans 8:34, NLT

I am a member of the body of Christ.

Now you are Christ's body, and individually
members of it.
—1 Corinthians 12:27, NASB

I have His anointing and seal over me.

Now it is God who makes both us and you
stand firm in Christ. He anointed us...
—2 Corinthians 1:21, NIV

I am protected from my enemy.

We know that no one who is born of God sins;
but He who was born of God keeps him, and
the evil one does not touch him.

—1 John 5:18, NASB

I am His workmanship and created for good.

For we are His workmanship, created in Christ
Jesus for good works, which God prepared be-
forehand so that we would walk in them.

—Ephesians 2:10, NASB

God has seated me with Him in the heavenly realms.

...and raised us up with Him, and seated us with
Him in the heavenly places in Christ Jesus...

—Ephesians 2:6, NASB

I have access to God through the Holy Spirit.

...for through Him we both have our access in
one Spirit to the Father.

—Ephesians 2:18, NASB

I know that He will use all things in my life for good.

And we know that God causes all things to work together for good to those who love God, to those who are called according to His purpose.
—Romans 8:28, NASB

I have confidence that He will continue to perfect and change me for good.

Being confident of this very thing, that he which hath begun a good work in you will perform it until the day of Jesus Christ...
—Philippians 1:6, KJV

I am His branch and He uses me to bear fruit.

Yes, I am the vine; you are the branches. Those who remain in me, and I in them, will produce much fruit. For apart from me you can do nothing.
—John 15:5, NLT

He does not give me fear, but His power, love, and a sound mind.

For God hath not given us the spirit of fear; but of power, and of love, and of a sound mind.
—2 Timothy 1:7, KJV

I have been anointed with God's power to be His witness.

> *...but you will receive power when the Holy Spirit has come upon you; and you shall be My witnesses both in Jerusalem, and in all Judea and Samaria, and even to the remotest part of the earth.*
> —Acts 1:8, NASB

I am given mercy and grace when I need it.

> *Therefore let us draw near with confidence to the throne of grace, so that we may receive mercy and find grace to help in time of need.*
> —Hebrews 4:16, NASB

I can do all things through the strength that Christ gives me.

> *I can do all things through Him who strengthens me.*
> —Philippians 4:13, NASB

The benefit of learning to affirm and encourage myself is twofold. You've probably heard it said that in order to love others, you must first love yourself. There is much truth to this. If I don't love myself, I have little capacity to love others. Love is affirming and encouraging. When I train myself to love and affirm myself, I'm training my mind to see the good in myself and others. When I affirm myself, I feel more confident. When I'm more confident, I'm more successful. When I'm successful, I'm happier. When I'm happy, I notice the negatives less often.

Have you ever noticed that when you're in a good mood, the little things just don't bother you as much? However, when you're in a bad mood already, all the little comments from others bother you much more. Did you know that you have the power to change this? You can take control over your mind to see the good instead of the negative.

The Bible tells me to take my thoughts captive. 2 Corinthians 10:5 says, *"We demolish arguments and every pretension that sets itself up against the knowledge of God, and take captive every thought to make it obedient to Christ"* (NIV). Demolish arguments! Wow, that's powerful. What about all those negative thoughts we allow our minds to dwell on? God is telling us to destroy them. But what does it mean to take our thoughts captive? It means to stop allowing them to control us. It means to make the negative thoughts prisoner instead of being a prisoner to the negative thoughts we've been dwelling on. It means to take prisoner the negative thoughts we have allowed to control us. So how do we do that?

God gave me a very poignant lesson one day. My husband and I had been arguing. The enemy was telling me that our marriage was a sham. I was having a pity party and dwelling on every negative thought possible. I was allowing myself to wallow in misery. However, I didn't know that I was allowing it. Of course I was upset. I'm sure you have had days like this, too.

Anyway, my kids would try to talk to me about their little problems. Of course their problems seemed little to me; I thought my marriage was over. Now, the truth is that my marriage wasn't over. We just had a little spat. I don't even remember what it was about. That's how insignificant it really was. But the enemy was globalizing it in my mind, and I let him. So I dwelt on all the negatives. Can you see how we allow the little things to take over? Well, I did.

Later, I had a client session, and I had to pull it together. I couldn't go and be the big counsellor to help someone else while I was in that state. I knew what to do: I prayed, I reminded myself of James 1:5, and I reminded God of James 1:5, just in case He'd forgotten His promise to me. I reminded myself that He is the counsellor and all I have to do is show up and be obedient to what He tells me to do or say. I knew I could do this, and of course He did show up, because He always does, because He is always faithful.

I felt better, but God chose to use this as a lesson. He showed me that, in fact, I had done this. I had chosen to overcome my miserable attitude to put my client first. Then He asked me why I didn't do that for my children.

Ooooh, big ouch. Seriously, was I that bad of a mother? No. Because God is always encouraging and affirming, He reminded me of all the truly wonderful things I have done for my children. However, He used this example to teach me that I *can* take my thoughts captive when I want or need to. I *can* choose to stop dwelling on negatives.

Furthermore, He asked me what good can come of all the times when I allow myself to mope and dwell on negative thoughts. How did it help me? Well, it doesn't help, of course. In fact, negativity breeds more negativity. I allowed myself to think even worse things about my husband, which only served to cause problems in my marriage. See how tricky the enemy is? He wants to destroy my marriage. Most of the time when I'm hurt or upset by my husband, it's due to a misunderstanding that is cleared up when I calmly discuss the situation with him. However, when I allow myself to dwell on the negatives and globalize everything, I don't treat him with respect—and then of course it turns into a big argument that could have been prevented through taking my thoughts captive.

Of course, it's not always so simple. Dwelling on the negative isn't always due to my husband or my perception that someone's done me wrong. There are valid issues that come up and hit us like a ton of bricks. I've had my share of those. However, the same principle holds true: I can choose to allow myself to dwell on the negatives or I can choose to release it to God and dwell on the positives.

You see, God doesn't just tell us not to think on the negatives. He tells us what to think on and how to overcome negativity. Philippians 4:6–9 says,

Do not be anxious about anything, but in every situation, by prayer and petition, with thanksgiving, present your requests to God. And the peace of God, which transcends all understanding, will guard your hearts and your minds in Christ Jesus.

Finally, brothers and sisters, whatever is true, whatever is noble, whatever is right, whatever is pure, whatever is lovely, whatever is admirable—if anything is excellent or praiseworthy—think about such things. Whatever you have learned or received or heard from me, or seen in me—put it into practice. And the God of peace will be with you. (NIV)

So we give it to God and thank Him. There's always much I can be thankful for, and you, too. I encourage you to start thinking of all you do have to be thankful for. Think of what is noble, and pure, and right, and lovely, and admirable. This is a great litmus test for our thoughts. When I'm worrying about what some person at church is thinking of me, is it pure? Is it noble? Is it admirable? Is it lovely? Hmmm, so I guess that would qualify as negative thinking. Or how about when I'm thinking about how rude and selfish someone is? How lovely and noble is that? Or when I'm putting myself down, is that right, pure, admirable, or praiseworthy? To criticize what God has created?

I encourage you to use this litmus test for your own negative self-talk. Take your thoughts captive. Encourage yourself. Affirm yourself. You don't need to wait for someone else to do it for you. Focus on your identity in Christ. This is your heritage. You have been grafted into the family of Christ. Romans 11:17 says,

> *But some of these branches from Abraham's tree—some of the people of Israel—have been broken off. And you Gentiles, who were branches from a wild olive tree, have been grafted in. So now you also receive the blessing God has promised Abraham and his children, sharing in the rich nourishment from the root of God's special olive tree.* (NLT)

This is who He says you are. So start living as though you believe it! Receive your truth.

Exercises

1. How are you an encourager?

_____

_____

_____

_____

_____

2. Is fear of man or fear of judgment a factor in your life? How so?

_____

_____

_____

_____

_____

3. Are you judgmental of others? Think about it and be honest with yourself.

_____

_____

_____

_____

_____

4. Are you able to take your thoughts captive? How?

_____

_____

_____

_____

_____

5. How do you affirm yourself? Or how will you do so going forward?

_____

_____

_____

_____

_____

7.

Your Emotional Bank Account

I HAVE HEARD IT SAID MANY TIMES THAT A RELATIONSHIP IS LIKE a bank account. There need to be deposits to balance out the withdrawals. We can share our hurts, joys, successes, and failures with good friends, knowing that they will be supportive and encouraging—or they'll just listen as we process our feelings. We of course do the same for them, and no one really needs to keep score. That's a comfortable relationship.

However, sometimes we have friends who seem to make a lot of withdrawals. You know the ones I'm talking about—the people who are always whining and complaining and crying on our shoulders, but never seem to take the time to listen to us. Do you find yourself avoiding these people? I certainly do. It can be very draining. These are not equal relationships. They aren't balanced accounts.

Of course, as a counsellor, I have relationships with my clients, but those are different. They're professional relationships. I don't expect my clients to reciprocate, and I usually only see them for an hour per week. I have the joy and fulfillment of seeing my clients work through their issues, improve, and come to new and healthier ways of coping. They come to me for help, to learn how to overcome. I love working with my clients. They're still balanced relationships, unlike the sort of people who only make withdrawals. These so-called friends only want to dump on me, and they rarely improve.

I'm also well aware that I have been guilty of being the perpetual withdrawer in some of my past relationships. Obviously, those relationships didn't turn out so well. Having this awareness has become a great checkpoint for me. I now make a point of reviewing my relationships every now and again to ensure I'm making deposits as well as withdrawals.

I have a very good friend who is my mentor, counsellor, supervisor, and much more. I often feel like I'm making all the withdrawals with her, but she frequently says the same thing to me. This is the best kind of relationship to have, as it is comfortable. Making deposits with her is so easy that I'm not even aware I'm doing it. If only it were that easy with my financial bank account!

So what about you? Do you put yourself down? Do you criticize yourself when you make a mistake? Do you have a need for perfection? Do you launch into tirades about how inept you are? Well, I've been guilty of all these things, and in my experience many people are.

I propose that you make an emotional bank account for yourself. You can do this on paper, or you can do it mentally. If this has been an ongoing issue for you, it will be much more helpful to actually do it on paper, or on your computer. You can download a simple ledger just as you do for your personal financial accounting. Once you've been doing this for a while, I think it'll become automatic and you will start to do it in your head. As I mentioned before, you need to build a new and healthy habit to replace old ways of thinking.

You don't need columns for taxes or any extras. This is a simple two-column ledger for yourself, between yourself. You're not dependent upon someone else for these affirmations. This is all about balancing your own negative self-talk and putdowns. Every time you put yourself down, put it in the withdrawals column. Then you have to balance the account, so make a deposit by acknowledging something good about yourself. This can be tricky, because you need to learn about yourself first.

What will work for a deposit? It has to actually work for it to be effective. For example, if I say to myself, "Oh, I'm so stupid!" obviously that is a withdrawal. If I then put in my deposit side, "No, you're not stupid!" I'm probably not actually going to be balanced, because I might not believe it. For me to say "I'm stupid," I probably had good reason to feel that way. It's going to take a bit more work to refute that lie. And it is a lie. The Bible tells me,

"I am fearfully and wonderfully made" (Psalm 139:14, NIV), so how can I be stupid?

Try making the following declarations:

- As a disciple, I am a friend of Jesus Christ (see John 15:15).
- I am free from condemnation (see Romans 8:1–2).
- I am assured that God works for my good in all circumstances (see Romans 8:28).

This works for me. I believe the Bible is the inerrant Word of God.

> *All scripture is given by inspiration of God, and is profitable for doctrine, for reproof, for correction, for instruction in righteousness...*
> —2 Timothy 3:16, KJV

> *Sanctify them through thy truth: thy word is truth.*
> —John 17:17, KJV

This makes for a very good deposit. I'm definitely balanced and can go forward confidently and emotionally healthy.

You need to make a list of what kinds of deposits will work for you for many different kinds of withdrawals.

What do you do to comfort yourself? That might be a good place to start. However, be careful, since simply comforting yourself might not actually balance your ledger. If a woman always goes shopping to make herself feel better after a fight, that is a comfort, but it doesn't necessarily absolve her of guilt. Having comforts that work for the tough stuff in life is good, but it's different from challenging the lies you tell yourself.

Many clients have told me that they tell themselves recurrent lies, and they've come to believe them. These are statements such as "I am unworthy," "I am unlovable," "I have no purpose," "I am worthless," etc. These are actual lies. All people are worthy of being loved. *"...for God bought you with a high price"* (1 Corinthians 6:20, NLT). A proper deposit will refute the lie.

Take some time to learn how to balance your emotional bank account. I have included a sample ledger at the end of this chapter to give you an idea of how to proceed. This is just a guide. Make yours balance for you.

Exercises

Make your own emotional bank account and start to use it regularly. There is a blank one attached that you may use, but I encourage you to copy several or make your own to fill in repeatedly until this has become your habit.

Sample Emotional Bank Account

Date	Withdrawals	Deposits
Sept. 4	I was mad at myself for sleeping in. I berated myself and said, "I am lazy."	I reminded myself that I was up very late looking after my sick child and that my body needed the rest. I am not lazy. I am a good mother.
Sept. 5	I had a disagreement with my husband. I told myself that our problems are always my fault. I'm ruining my marriage.	I reminded myself that I'm human and do make mistakes, but I don't intentionally hurt anyone. It is not always my fault. I will discuss the situation with him calmly until we come to a resolution. I know that he loves me and I love him.
Sept. 8	I dropped my favourite cup and broke it. I told myself that I'm clumsy and ruin everything.	I remembered that my hands were slippery because I was making dinner. It was just one of those things. I'm not clumsy. I will buy myself a new favourite cup.
Sept. 12	I forgot that I had a test for my class, and I did not do well. I told myself that I'm so stupid and should have remembered to study.	I recognize that I'm a busy wife and mother, trying to work and also better myself through education. I couldn't have studied because I was so busy. I can ask to retake the test or be okay with not receiving a perfect mark. I will schedule time for myself in order to allow myself to study and do the things that are important for me.

Blank Sample Emotional Bank Account

Date	Withdrawals	Deposits

8

Changing the Habit of Insufferiority

YES, THAT'S RIGHT, I SAID "HABIT." OUR INSECURITIES BECOME habits in our lives, and we allow ourselves to live by them. It is a habit to put oneself down. It is a habit to feel inferior to others. It is a habit to see ourselves as inadequate. Your low self-esteem becomes a habitual response.

It was my habit to view things negatively in my life. Yes, this was modelled for me, but it's my responsibility to seek truth and change my outcomes through trust in God. The enemy worked to prove this lie to me. He conspired to show me that things would turn out negatively. I received this lie and set my expectations accordingly. What about you? Do you create self-fulfilling prophecies of negativity in your life? Do you give the enemy permission to work these lies in your life by professing negativity? Are you ready to change these habits?

You may have heard of CBT (cognitive behaviour therapy). The word cognitive refers to the way we think.

Behaviours are the ways in which we act and respond to things. Basically, our behaviour is ruled by our thinking. If we think negatively of ourselves, we will respond negatively to ourselves and, perhaps inadvertently, invite negative responses from others.

If I tell you I'm going to do something but don't actually believe I can do it, I will convey doubt in your mind, too. When you go to a sales presentation, you're often compelled to buy things you had no intention of buying. This is because the salesperson has such a great belief in their product that it comes across and impacts your decision-making. They're excited about their product, and this excitement is contagious. In the same way, negative promotion is contagious.

Do you negatively promote yourself? I know that I've often done so in the past. In my twisted thinking, I was actually seeking encouragement from others, but it doesn't happen if we don't believe in ourselves first. My negativity encouraged more negativity. Then, when I didn't receive the affirmation and encouragement I desired and hoped for, I interpreted this as confirmation that I was right to doubt myself in the first place. Do you see how tricky the enemy is? What an awful downward spiral! It's time to take control of your own thinking and change your outcomes.

Step One

In order to change our outcomes, we need to change our thinking, our cognitions. This will then change our behaviours.

The first step is to own your own feelings. Have you ever heard someone say, "You make me so angry"? Have you ever made such a statement? The truth is that you cannot "make" me angry. I cannot "make" you angry. Your behaviour may trigger me toward anger, but I then have a choice as to how I respond to it.

Much of the time, we're not consciously aware that we're making a choice, but we are, and we have the ability and responsibility to work toward changing the responses we don't like in ourselves. As long as I hold you accountable for my angry outburst, I'll never change my behaviours, and they will affect me negatively until I do. I need to own my anger and recognize that I'm responsible for my behaviour. So do you. Once I recognize this, then and only then can I work toward changing my behaviour. It doesn't matter what others do; they are responsible for their own behaviour the same as I am.

Yes, this is hard. I never promised it would be easy, and neither did God. In John 16:33, Jesus said, *"I have told you all this so that you may have peace in me. Here on earth you will have many trials and sorrows. But take heart, because I have overcome the world"* (NLT).

So own your feelings and reactions. Recognize that you are responsible for them.

Step Two

In Chapter Six, I wrote about how I was able to overcome my negative spiral to be there for a client, but I had believed myself incapable of doing the same at home. God taught me about taking my thoughts captive. You need to take your negative thoughts captive in order to overcome your negative thinking and insufferiority.

Make a list of all the negative thoughts and assessments you make about yourself. You might already have this list from the exercises in previous chapters.

Step Three

Now refute each lie with truth. Find scriptures that align truth with the lies you've been telling yourself. Write them out on cue cards or sticky notes and keep them where you'll see them regularly. This way, you can practice stating truth instead of the lies you've told yourself for years. I put them on my bathroom mirror so I can see them every day while I'm getting ready—brushing my teeth, putting on makeup, etc. I put them on the bulletin board in my office, or right in front of me at my computer. Some people put them on the dashboards of their cars. (For safety reasons, maybe don't use lengthy ones for the car.) Find what will work best for you.

I asked my daughter to decorate and make a pretty border around some of my favourite scriptures about our identity in Christ, which she then framed. We put it in our living room. I've also placed it in several other strategic places around my home so that the truth is right there, visible when I'm in my doubting mode and allowing negative thoughts to take control. We need to make it easy for ourselves to see and remember the truth, because when we're struggling we won't have the energy or motivation to go searching for it. Make it accessible and in your face.

Practice repeating the truth when you're calm. Don't wait until you're upset or having a pity party or busy beating yourself up. This is a common mistake. We think we'll do it the next time we're going through a tough time, but the truth is that we're always struggling with insufferiority. When we're in a real funk, dwelling on everything negatively, we don't have the emotional strength to fight it. However, if we've practiced handling it when we are calm, we'll be better armed for the tough times.

If you're having trouble finding Scripture to refute the lies, ask God to help you. You can use the examples I cited in Chapter Six. I often ask my clients, "How does God see you?" Many suffer from low self-esteem, and they find answers as they ponder and pray about this question. While I was struggling with some issues one day, I asked God the same question. His response was, "If you saw yourself as I see you, you would be too proud. You would then struggle with arrogance." I was shocked by His response, but I felt good, too. It was a very positive affirmation! It also left me wondering what to do with it. It was definitely one of those gems I knew could come only from God. Truly, it propelled me to seek and trust in Him more for everything, which I'm sure was His desired response from me. I'm so grateful that I am chosen, predestined, and blessed. I'm more grateful now that He's helped me make the choice to be counted as part of His elect. I have been grafted into the vine, and He bears fruit in me. Wow!

What is God saying to you?

Step Four

What we're going to do is build new habits in your life. I've heard it said that it takes three weeks to form a new habit. I have since read an article that refuted this. The truth is that we're all different, so you'll need to do some self-evaluation to find out exactly how long it will take for you. However, I believe three weeks is about the average.

Many of us will notice or recognize that our bad habits form much faster than the good ones. Is that because it's not hard to build the bad ones as we aren't working at them? Perhaps so, but investigate yourself to learn how long it will take to form a new habit in your life. For the sake of argument, I'm going to use three weeks here.

You probably have a habit of brushing your teeth daily. This was hopefully a habit formed when you were a child. You didn't automatically do it. Likely your parents told you to do so repeatedly until it became a habit that you incorporated into your daily routine. You also likely dress and comb your hair on a daily basis. You're probably not even conscious of doing these things much of the time. It has become habitual.

When I was first learning to drive, I had to concentrate every time I got behind the wheel of a car. Was my seat adjusted properly? Was the rear-view mirror adjusted so that I could comfortably see what was behind me while driving? Was my seatbelt on? What about the side mirrors? I was conscious of putting the transmission into drive. I thought about shoulder-checking and using my signal lights. When I stopped to park, I had to focus on remembering to ensure I had put the transmission back into park. I had to think about turning off the lights, which did not happen automatically when I learned to drive. Now, these things have all become so habitual that there are times when I don't consciously remember the drive to or from somewhere. The habits I formed as a teenager are ingrained in me. If you drive, I'm sure you can relate.

I have some of my best talks with God in the shower. Why do you think this is? I'm alone, without interruption, and don't need to use my brain to go about the requirements of washing my hair and body. I have a routine there, too, that I automatically go through.

By the same token, I wasn't aware of my habitual responses when I used to dwell negatively. I didn't even realize it when I had negative responses to other people. I had to work very hard to break those habits. They still like to sneak in occasionally, but I'm aware of them now. I recognize when I slip and I know how to change it. Why? Because I've worked very hard to break the old habits and form new ones.

As I mentioned before, God never just tells us not to do something. He always provides a positive alternative. Philippians 4:6 says, *"Do not be anxious about anything, but in every situation, by prayer and petition, with thanksgiving, present your requests to God"* (NIV). See, Paul tells us not to be anxious, and then he tells us what to do. He tells us clearly to pray. He gives us God's promise of peace: *"And the peace of God, which transcends all understanding, will guard your hearts and your minds in Christ Jesus"* (Philippians 4:7, NIV). He goes further, telling us what to focus our minds on:

> *Finally, brothers and sisters, whatever is true, whatever is noble, whatever is right, whatever is pure, whatever is lovely, whatever is admirable—if anything is excellent or praiseworthy—think about such things.*
> —Philippians 4:8, NIV

Did you see that? The Bible actually tells us how to take our thoughts captive and what to "think on." Are the things you profess about yourself true, noble, right, pure, lovely, admirable, and praiseworthy? This is what you're commanded to profess.

This isn't going to be automatic at first. We'll have to work hard to change our habits. But if you know that it takes three weeks to form a new habit, the end is in sight.

A few years ago, I started going to the gym. Honestly, I had thought about doing so for years before that, but it took me a long time to build up the motivation to actually do it. Once I actually joined a gym, I had to work really hard to force myself to go. I just didn't feel like going many days. Who am I kidding, I didn't feel like going *any* day. I had to work very hard to force myself to go.

However, I did feel like going once this habit was formed. In fact, my body had grown so accustomed to it that my muscles literally ached on days when I wasn't able to go. Do you think this propelled me to find ways to go no matter what? Yes! I had many obligations and family responsibilities keeping me from it, but I worked hard to overcome these reasons, because the desire became so great. It's certainly much easier to justify doing something that's good for me.

The point is that I had built a habit that hadn't been natural for me previously, and then it became an automatic part of my routine to head to the gym after work.

My car instinctively seems to drive that way now instead of heading home.

It might feel weird and unnatural at first. This is normal. Our automatic negative responses actually feel comfortable because they're the norm, the habit we have formed. I've heard that if an elephant is chained to a post from the time it is young, you don't even need to have the chain attached to the post when it's an adult; the elephant will not even attempt to walk away. It's free, but it stays captive. We have stayed captive to our insufferiority, too, and we are free!

Galatians 5:1 says, *"So Christ has truly set us free. Now make sure that you stay free, and don't get tied up again in slavery..."* (NLT). We have allowed ourselves to be enslaved to insufferiority, but we can break those bonds and be free. We have become comfortable in doing things the same way. Now we need to force ourselves to build new habitual responses until this new way becomes the norm—until this new way becomes comfortable. Yes, it will become automatic and comfortable if we truly work hard at it. It's doable when we realize we can force ourselves to do anything for three weeks. As we become aware of our negativity, we'll have to force ourselves to change our responses for the period of time it takes to build the new habits. It absolutely will become an automatic response to profess truth if we work through the tough times.

Samantha originally came to me to work on her anger. It was ruining her life, her marriage, and having a terrible impact on her children. She didn't want to be that way. She loved her family, but her anger would overtake her, and she knew she was destroying her family. We worked on the roots of her anger. She had come from a dysfunctional family, which had a detrimental impact on her life. We worked through inner healing on much pain from her childhood. However, we also worked on her angry responses and outbursts. Samantha worked very hard to change her habits, and was having success, but she commented frequently about how difficult it was. She felt like she had to always "be on." It wasn't the natural response, and it took so much effort. However, Samantha persisted and stopped herself from the automatic responses that had been her norm. She continually reminded herself of truth and worked to overcome the negativity she had been professing previously.

It was one of my greatest joys to hear later that her new controlled and positive responses became automatic. She was loving and kind and positive as the norm. She had overcome her negativity and transformed into a new person. She was free from the bondage Satan had put upon her. She was living the life Christ had created her to live. I love my job. What an absolute joy and fulfillment to have witnessed Christ work this change in Samantha.

This will be your outcome, too. Don't despair when it gets tough, for there is light at the end of the tunnel.

If you slip occasionally, that's okay. We're human. Don't allow the enemy to beat you up, and most definitely don't beat yourself up over it. That's where defeat enters in. You are not a defeatist anymore. You are a new person in Christ, created for good.

Tell yourself the truth every day. When you wake up in the morning, profess God's truth about who you are. When you lie down at night, thank God for His great love and all He has done for you and given you. Put your focus on the positives and it will become your new outlook. Praise Him when you are angry, sad, and feeling defeated.

Isaiah 61:3 tells us,

To all who mourn in Israel, he will give a crown of beauty for ashes, a joyous blessing instead of mourning, festive praise instead of despair. In their righteousness, they will be like great oaks that the Lord has planted for his own glory. (NLT)

This is truth. It's hard to discipline myself to praise God when I'm struggling, but it absolutely works. I cannot be downcast when I start to praise God. I cannot put myself down when I remind myself of His great sacrifice for me. In tougher times, I always remind myself that He uses everything for good.

Romans 8:28 says, *"And we know that in all things God works for the good of those who love him, who have been called according to his purpose"* (NIV). So even when I screw up—and yes, I still do that a lot—God uses my mistakes for good. When I say something nasty and immediately taste that awful foot in my mouth, I remind myself that God will use it for good because His Word says so. Yes, I will likely have to apologize, but sometimes I know it's never enough. Once I've said something, it cannot be taken back. I cringe every time I think of it later or see the person I said it to. So I have to repent of it, receive forgiveness from God—whether the recipient forgives me or not—and then forgive myself.

God often uses these times to teach us valuable lessons, and He uses them in the other person's life, too. I don't always understand it, but God has delivered me and set me free. If I continue to dwell on the mistake and negativity, I'm not moving forward in what God is asking of me. David moved forward, and that's what God wants us to do, too.

Furthermore, remember that in all our endeavours, it is often two steps forward, one step back. You will have setbacks, and that is okay. Allow yourself to be human. I still have days when I'm struggling and *choose* to wallow for a while. It sounds ridiculous, doesn't it? Why would I choose to wallow? Well, it doesn't always make sense, but the biggest difference is that I now acknowledge that I'm choosing it. I don't blame my family or circumstance. I recognize that for this day or time, I'm allowing myself to be down. I work hard not to allow it to affect those around me. So I might take that day to be by myself, because I know that negativity is contagious and I don't want to spread it to others. During these times, I'm also well aware of what I have to do to overcome it, and know that I will do so tomorrow.

Sometimes I don't feel strong enough. Sometimes I struggle under the weight of attack from the enemy. During these times, I allow God to minister to me. He comforts me and reminds me that when I am weak, He is strong (2 Corinthians 12:10). I remind myself that God doesn't expect me to be strong all the time. I recognize His promise to me in Deuteronomy 31:6:

> *Be strong and courageous. Do not be afraid or terrified because of them, for the Lord your God goes with you; he will never leave you nor forsake you.* (NIV)

He loves me as I am—always. He loves you as you are—always. He loves you right now, even while you're still struggling with insufferiority. He sees you as the finished picture of wholeness and living in freedom, as He created you to be. He equips you with His armour (Ephesians 6:10–17). He has given you all that you need to succeed.

My brother regularly asks his children, "What are you?" The response he has trained them to say is "I am a success!" They roll their eyes at him, but deep down they believe it and know it to be true because they've been raised with this motto. They have prophesied truth over themselves from a very young age. What a great legacy to give his children.

A "success" can mean many different things. One can be successful in business, education, spirituality, and life in general. But whatever connotation one might put upon it, it is always positive. We grow to be whatever we believe we can be.

Some of you might remember the old TV sitcom *Sanford and Son*. The father always called his son "Dummy." In one of the episodes, the son said that he'd thought his name was "Dummy Sanford" until he was six years old. How sad! This was only a TV show, but this kind of joking happens frequently in our lives, and it's not funny.

I used to sell registered educational savings plans, and I learned of a statistic showing that children who grow up with provision made by their parents for post-secondary education most always use it. This is because they know they can. They have grown up believing in the possibility, and so they fulfill it. What do you believe you can do? What will you start to believe you can do? Start professing over yourself the things you want to do, and you'll start to believe them. It really is that simple. No, it's not easy, but the concept is simple. Once you embrace it, and start living it, you'll be free. Ask God what He wants you to profess over yourself. He is always faithful to answer.

Matthew 7:9–11 says,

You parents—if your children ask for a loaf of bread, do you give them a stone instead? Or if they ask for a fish, do you give them a snake? Of course not! So if you sinful people know how to give good gifts to your children, how much more will your heavenly Father give good gifts to those who ask him. (NLT)

So ask Him.

For God's gifts and his call can never be withdrawn.

—Romans 11:29, NLT

Exercises

1. How will you be accountable and own your own feelings? Make a plan.

_____

_____

_____

_____

2.   Make a list of all the negative thoughts and assessments you make about yourself.

_____

_____

_____

_____

_____

3.   Now refute each lie with truth. Find scriptures that align truth with the lies you've been telling yourself.

_____

_____

_____

_____

_____

4.   Make reminders for yourself in order to change your habits.

_____

_____

_____

_____

_____

5.   How will you reward yourself every time you successfully utilize the truth instead of the lies you used to profess?

_____

_____

_____

_____

_____

9.

Accepting God's Love

Once again you will have compassion on us.
You will trample our sins under your feet and
throw them into the depths of the ocean!
—Micah 7:19, NLT

As you start to overcome your insufferiority, I encourage you to embrace who you are. Allow yourself to accept God's amazing, unconditional love.

Last night, my friend, who is a strong spiritual mentor, was going through a rough time. She confided to me that she didn't even know if she was a Christian anymore. I knew she was just venting, but she obviously needed some encouragement. She didn't "feel" God's love, but it doesn't mean it wasn't there. I asked if she knew I love her and she said yes. I realized at that point that I could relate at times, yet how sad it is that sometimes it's easier to receive love from a human than from God. As I thought about it, God pointed out that we struggle when we feel imperfect. We know that our friends, family, and other people in our lives are imperfect as well, so we know they can relate to and understand our imperfections. Therefore, it is perhaps easier to receive their love. But God is perfect, so we sometimes think He can't possibly understand or love us.

What a deception this is from the enemy. God understands us most and loves us most—more than we can possibly understand.

> *How great is our Lord! His power is absolute!*
> *His understanding is beyond comprehension!*
> —Psalm 147:5, NLT

> *For just as the heavens are higher than the earth, so my ways are higher than your ways and my thoughts higher than your thoughts.*
> —Isaiah 55:9, NLT

He loves me in spite of my imperfections. He loved me while I was still a sinner. Perhaps that's the key; I often still feel like I'm a sinner, but I think I shouldn't be for God to accept me. The truth is that He sent His Son so that I could feel loved and accepted as I am.

> *Understand, therefore, that the Lord your God is indeed God. He is the faithful God who keeps his covenant for a thousand generations and*

lavishes his unfailing love on those who love him and obey his commands.

— Deuteronomy 7:9, NLT

Have you never heard? Have you never understood? The Lord is the everlasting God, the Creator of all the earth. He never grows weak or weary. No one can measure the depths of his understanding.

— Isaiah 40:28, NLT

I have loved you, my people, with an everlasting love. With unfailing love I have drawn you to myself.

— Jeremiah 31:3, NLT

If you haven't received Jesus as your personal Saviour, I encourage you to do so now. Hope, health, and healing are available through Christ Jesus.

For this is how God loved the world: He gave his one and only Son, so that everyone who believes in him will not perish but have eternal life.

— John 3:16, NLT

The thief comes only to steal and kill and destroy; I have come that they may have life, and have it to the full.

— John 10:10, NIV

But God demonstrates his own love for us in this: While we were still sinners, Christ died for us.

—Romans 5:8, NIV

Jesus answered, "I am the way and the truth and the life. No one comes to the Father except through me."

—John 14:6, NIV

If you declare with your mouth, "Jesus is Lord," and believe in your heart that God raised him from the dead, you will be saved.

—Romans 10:9, NLT

If you want to know God's love and experience His life to the fullest, pray this prayer:

Dear Lord Jesus Christ, I repent of the things I have done wrong in my life. I ask your forgiveness and commit to follow you for the rest of my days. Thank you for dying on the cross for me and setting me free from my sins. Please come into my life and fill me with your Holy Spirit. Thank you for your promises to be with me forever. I now receive your forgiveness and your healing. I receive your love. Thank you, Lord Jesus. Amen.

Exercises

1.   Do you accept God's unconditional love for you? How? What does this mean to you?

_____

_____

_____

_____

_____

2.   Have you accepted Jesus as your personal Lord and Saviour? Take some time to do so now or reconfirm your commitment to Him. What does this mean in your life?

_____

_____

_____

_____

_____

3. How will your life be different, having worked through your insufferiority?

_____

_____

_____

_____

_____

4. How will you refute the enemy's attack when he tries to steal your healing?

_____

_____

_____

_____

_____

10

Embrace Your Individuality

ONE DAY I NOTICED A LITTLE FLOWER ON OUR LAWN. I WAS STRUCK by how beautifully it stood out. The grass was a sea of sameness, each blade fitting in with the rest of the crowd, like so many of us want to do in life. We don't want to feel different, weird, out of place. Yet this little flower poked up so proudly. It was a reminder to me of God's beautiful creation. If it were in a field of flowers all the same, it wouldn't be noticeable. It wouldn't have touched me with its own uniqueness. The grass on its own is nothing special, but this little flower was a picture of hope, light, and radiant décor. God has created you as His décor. So shine for Him.

As you embrace the new confident, sufficient, adequate, and secure person God created you to be, embrace your uniqueness, too. Ask Him what purposes He wants to accomplish through you. If someone had told me ten years ago that I would write a book, I would have said they were crazy. Writing a book wasn't my goal, or even on my radar. Then something happened. God dropped ideas and inspiration into my heart. He caused the message to burn within me until I realized that I had to share it. He gave me the courage to believe in the possibility, the daring to go forth and the confidence to believe in the capability He had given me. He gave me the willingness to trust in Him and His power to make it happen. He helped me to be obedient to the call He put on me. Then He taught me patience to wait for His timing to make it happen.

Learn to rest in Him for all your endeavours.

Trust and obey,
For there's no other way
To be happy in Jesus,
But to trust and obey.[2]

This famous hymn rings in my heart.

God has been speaking to me about His rest. He gives me a holiday to rest from all the weights I carry, and then He asks me why I pick them up again after I come home. He has reminded me that He's carrying them, and when I trust in Him, all is well.

He gave me the analogy of a map. Just as I see a destination on a map, He gives me glimpses of the future He has for me. On the map, I have an idea of how

---

2 John H. Sammis, "Trust and Obey," 1887.

long it should take me to get from A to B, but I don't always allow time for the roadblocks, detours, and delays along the way. He has told me that I automatically assign timelines to the maps He gives me, but it's not always His timing. As on the roadmap, He doesn't tell me all the bumps in the road that I will face. However, He has reminded me that when I slow down for the bumps, I can glide over them gently. They only hurt when I'm trying to speed through them. He has told me to slow down and enjoy the ride, as there are blessings that I miss in my haste. I will reach my promised land by allowing Him to take me there. He doesn't need my help.

I pray that this message has blessed you and that you are free of the burden of insufferiority.

Who Am I?

I am the child who lay awake in bed at night, afraid to go to sleep in fear of what harm may come.

I am the tween who cried herself to sleep because she was certain she wasn't as good as others and that no one could ever love her.

I am the teen who left home at sixteen, and on her night off from work would hide in her apartment with the lights off so no one would know she didn't have a party to go to.

I am the young woman who married for all the wrong reasons and ended up a divorced Christian, riddled with guilt, shame, and condemnation.

I am the woman who let judgment hold her back from doing what God asked—some of the judgment real, but much of it imagined.

I am the woman who ignored the phone calls of concerned friends because I didn't believe anyone could truly care about me.

I am the woman who would tiptoe to the door to look through the peephole to see who was there, then hide silently until they gave up and left.

I am the woman who allowed depression and anxiety to control her life and steal her joy.

I am a woman saved by grace.

I am a woman who knows the mighty healing touch of Jesus.

I am a Christian who has backslidden many times, and hurt people in ways that I can't fix.

I am a woman who knows the power of God's forgiveness, even when man can't.

I am a woman who is privileged to be used of God only because I have prayed, *"Here am I. Send me!"* (Isaiah 6:8, NIV)—not because I'm worthy, but because He is.

I am a woman who is blessed!

To contact the author, visit
www.findingfreedomcounselling.ca